Sing in Exultation!

"Christmas carols aren't just picturesque; they contain deep Christian teaching. In this little book, Jonathan Landry Cruse organizes twenty-five carol excerpts into an Advent calendar of reflections, each ornamented with Scripture and prayer. Let this be your guide through the month of December, as you treasure up the mystery of the incarnation and ponder it in your heart."

Josh Bauder, composer

"The Apostle Paul encourages us to sing in the Spirit with understanding. In this short book, Jonathan helps us to do just that, as he explains the meaning behind the words of our favorite (and now too familiar) Advent hymns and Christmas carols. This book will help you tune your heart (and mind) to the melody (and mystery) of the gospel, expressed so beautifully in the songs we sing each Advent and Christmas season."

Jonny Gibson, associate professor of Old Testament, Westminster Theological Seminary, Philadelphia

"Each year, the carols of Christmas sound in our ears, even as their words fill our mouths. Yet, the great aim of these carols is left undone if that is where they remain; their message is meant to fill our hearts. Jonathan Cruse's Christmas devotional, *Sing in Exultation!*, promotes this great end with brief and encouraging explanations, searching questions, and poignant prayers. Be prepared to have your understanding of famous Christmas carols expanded and your worship of Whom they sing enflamed."

Jason Helopoulos, pastor, University Reformed Church, Michigan and author, *The Promise* and *A Neglected Grace*

"A rare treat: a devotional that is both rich in content and manageable for daily use! Christmas is a time for singing. This little work will help individuals and families see that the good news woven into our favorite carols is both biblical and heart-warming. A wonderful way to sing your way through Advent."

Jonty Rhodes, minister, Christ Church Central, Leeds, UK

Sing in Exultation!

A Christmas Devotional

Exploring Our Favorite Carols

JONATHAN LANDRY CRUSE

10 Publishing
a division of 10ofthose.com

British Library Cataloguing in Publication Data
A record for this book is available from the British Library

US: 978-1-914966-89-7
UK: 978-1-83728-010-0

Designed by Jude May
Cover image © Cris | Adobe Stock

Printed in Denmark

10Publishing, a division of 10ofthose.com
Unit C, Tomlinson Road, Leyland, PR25 2DY, England
Email: info@10ofthose.com
Website: www.10ofthose.com

1 3 5 7 10 8 6 4 2

For Abby and the Jackson crew,
May this enrich your celebration of the birth of Christ.

And to Him who was made flesh and dwelt among us.

Contents

Introduction

One of the (many) wonderful things about Christmastime is that it gets us to do something we can be pretty reticent to do any other time of the year: sing together! The holidays can pry open our otherwise shy vocal cords and get us *fa-la-la-la-la*-ing with the best of them. Singing Christmas carols, for many, is one of the most beloved aspects of the season. As indispensable as hall-decking, light-stringing, or gift-giving, it wouldn't be Christmas without carol-singing.

Admittedly, there are a host of ditties about bullied reindeer, winter wonderlands, and rocking around Christmas trees, but most of the well-known songs of the season are actually packed with scriptural language and rich theology. This is a blessing. What other time of year do we find the characters in our favorite TV shows singing, "Glory to the newborn King!" or hear, "With the angels let us sing Alleluias" blaring out of the radio? When else might a non-Christian neighbor saunter into a nearby church and declare, "Joy to the world the Lord is come!"?

Realistically, many people at Christmas do not believe the words they are singing. Others believe the words, but do not fully understand them. Even those of us who have been believers for a while can get caught up in the excitement and sentimentality of the season and not pay close attention to the words we are singing. What does "rest ye merry" mean, after all? Or, "Word of the Father, late in flesh appearing"? In one carol, Charles Wesley says that Jesus is "risen with healing in His wings"—where did he get that language from, and what in the world does it mean?

The Apostle Paul said that we must "sing with our minds" (1 Cor. 14:15). Words that are sung with no understanding, even if sung in God's direction, fall flat before the Lord. This little book aims to unpack some of the best lines from the best carols, not only so we might better appreciate the meaning of the hymn, but the meaning of Christmas, too.

The carols are arranged in the book so that we start with the first prediction of Christ's coming and end with the hope of His second coming. So as you work through these twenty-five reflections you will be covering the Christmas story as told throughout all of Scripture. Our carols cover it all: Old Testament prophecies ("Let All Mortal Flesh Keep Silence"), angelic announcements ("Angels We Have Heard on High"), first visits to the Christ-child ("As with Gladness Men of Old"), and even powerful applications of how we should respond to the incarnation ("In the Bleak Mid-winter").

So, how should you use this little book? There are a number of ways. If you want to enjoy an overview of the importance of Christmas provided by some of our best carols, simply read it from beginning to end. This will take you through the biblical story of the promise and fulfillment of Christ's coming in a brief, albeit rich, way. If you are new to Christianity, you may be surprised at how much of the Christmas story you already know simply from the lyrics you have heard and sung over the years!

The book is also structured to be a helpful daily devotional in the season of advent leading up to Christmas. Each day covers a single verse from a carol. I would highly recommend singing this, especially if you are using the devotional with your family, though you could read it, too. Perhaps listening to a version online would be helpful if you're unfamiliar with the tune—or your family is reluctant to sing (it's okay—join in. No one will make fun of you!). We have put together a

Spotify playlist to make searching for the carols easier. You can access this by scanning the QR code below.

A short reflection follows each carol, exploring its biblical truth and significance, while always providing a point or two of application. If you want to meditate on the topics further, each chapter has suggested further reading and some questions to prompt more reflection or discussion. Finally, a prayer is provided for you. Feel free to let those words serve as your own prayer to God, or you may be moved to use your own words. In either case, the important thing is that these reflections, and the great carols they are based on, serve as a means of treasuring up God's amazing promises and purposes in our hearts—just like Mary (Lk. 2:51).

Scan here for a Spotify playlist to use alongside these devotions.

DECEMBER 1:

"Far As the Curse Is Found"

No more let sins and sorrows grow,
Nor thorns infest the ground;
He comes to make His blessings flow
Far as the curse is found.

–"Joy to the World!" Isaac Watts

Christmas begins with a curse. While sounding counterintuitive to a season that is supposed to be merry and bright, it's nevertheless true. After all, why did Jesus Christ come to earth in the first place? He came to "seek and to save the lost" (Lk. 19:10). We could say He was on a rescue mission—He came to rescue sinners under the cruel curse of sin and death.

"Joy to the World!" takes us back to the effects of Adam and Eve's first sin, which plunged both them and all of humanity into this curse. God pronounces in Genesis 3 that because Adam and Eve disobeyed their Maker, life would not be easy for them any longer. "Cursed is the ground because of you," He solemnly tells Adam. "In pain you shall eat of it all the days of your life; thorns and thistles it shall bring forth for you; and you shall eat the plants of the field" (vv. 17–18). The image is no longer of a luscious and enjoyable garden, but of frustrating and painful weeds and brambles.

Have you ever experienced the frustration of seemingly pointless work? Once, a church member and I carved out a whole day to sand down the front doors of the church and give them a fresh coat of red paint. We started early and then worked in the hot July sun until almost dinner, putting on two coats. It wasn't until we finally stepped away from the doors and looked back from the road that we noticed something we couldn't see up close: the paint hadn't dried the scarlet red we had intended. It was bright pink! We knew in an instant we would have to do the work all over again. My friend turned to me and said, shaking his head, "Thorns and thistles, thorns and thistles."

A bad paint job is the least of our problems. We feel the effects of sin every day: anger, violence, betrayal, injustice. We hear of it on the news, we experience it in our homes, we sense it even in our own hearts. We know that the world—and we along with it—doesn't work the way it's meant to. We no longer live in the blessed Garden of Eden. We live now where "sins and sorrows grow"—trapped in the thorny prison of the fallen world.

But then a rescue! That is what is so glorious about Christmas, but of course the good news isn't good if we don't first recognize the bad news. We live in a world of sin and sorrow, at every single turn, *but* Jesus has come to change all of that, and to "make His blessings flow" wherever "the curse is found."

Pray: *Father, I thank You that You don't leave us in our sin, though we deserve it. I praise You for Your rescuing grace, which sent Jesus to transform the curse of sin into the blessing of salvation. In His name I pray. Amen.*

Reflect:

Read Genesis 3.

- Think of a time when you were particularly discouraged and laid low by the effects of sin and suffering. How can such low points recalibrate your understanding of the gospel?
- In what ways do we now see the blessings of Christ in the midst of sin's curse, and in what ways do we still await further redemption?

DECEMBER 2:

"Ransom Captive Israel"

O come, O come, Emmanuel,
And ransom captive Israel
That mourns in lonely exile here
Until the Son of God appear.
Rejoice! Rejoice! Emmanuel
Shall come to you, O Israel.

–"O Come, O Come Emmanuel," traditional, translation by J. M. Neale

Both the words and melody of this carol do a remarkable job portraying the dark distress felt by the nation of Israel in their time of "lonely exile." Despite many warnings, the people had rejected God and as a result He allowed their enemies to conquer them. Many had been taken into a foreign land but ached to return. This carol's minor key and long, plaintive notes express how "captive Israel" must have felt as they were far from home, and far from the covenant blessings of God.

But that was then and this is now. We might wonder whether it's even an appropriate song for us to sing as New Covenant believers. Is it appropriate to identify as "Israel"? It is. In fact, the Apostle Paul calls the church "the Israel of God" (Gal. 6:16). The church is now the people of God—the true Israel. And while most Western Christians haven't experienced national upheaval like the ancient Israelites, we do know of the captivating power of sin. Satan is a far worse prison warden than any Egyptian pharaoh or Babylonian or Assyrian tyrant. And though Christ has defeated the *power* of sin over us, we have yet to be rescued from the *presence* of sin. This carol helps remind us that we should "mourn" the fact that we are still far from our heavenly home.

Do you mourn over your sin? Do you grieve over the sins of others, and the suffering that it all causes? So often we can become calloused to the reality of sin in and around us. We become far too familiar with this world and we get comfortable here, rather than longing for our true home and for pure hearts. Christians who do not grieve sin and its effects and who are too settled in this world have some major reprioritizing to do

While this carol reminds us to mourn, it also calls us to rejoice. Why? Because "Emmanuel shall come to you, O Israel." It is Emmanuel—"God with us"—and Emmanuel alone who can answer our great need. When He comes to be with us, all sin and sorrow will flee away. This was Israel's hope under the Old Covenant, and it is also the church's hope under the New Covenant as we await Christ's second coming. But we have *even more* reason to sing with joyful confidence than they, because we live this side of the first appearance of the Son of God. "He appeared in order to take away sins" (1 Jn. 3:5). Truly, we could sing, "Emmanuel *has* come to you"! And since He has come once, we can be confident He will come again.

Pray: *Lord, forgive me for the times I feel at home in this world and forget that actually I am destined for something much greater and better. Speed the return of Christ, so that I might live with Him in glory forevermore. Amen.*

Reflect:

Read Exodus 2:23–25.

- How does Israel's historic captivity help us to understand humanity's plight?
- Do you cry out like Israel for rescue, or do you find yourself feeling at home in this world? What steps can you take to love the world less and long for heaven more?

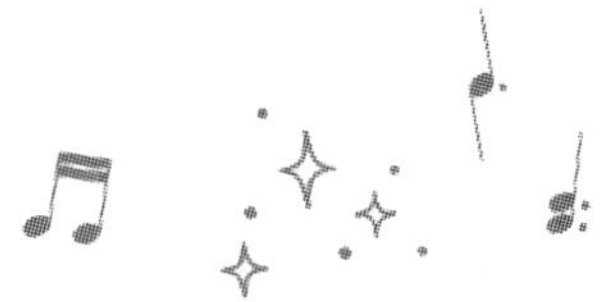

DECEMBER 3:

"Of Jesse's Lineage Coming"

Lo, how a rose e'er blooming
From tender stem hath sprung,
Of Jesse's lineage coming,
As men of old have sung.
It came, a flow'ret bright,
Amid the cold of winter, when half-spent was the night.

–"Lo, How a Rose E'er Blooming," traditional, translation by Theodore Baker

The imagery in this carol is unquestionably rich and vivid, but it's also somewhat confusing. Are we singing about a flower, after all? No—we are singing about Jesus! Standing behind the poetry is a biblical metaphor found in numerous places throughout the Old Testament. One such place would be Isaiah 11:

"There shall come forth a shoot from the stump of Jesse, and a branch from his roots shall bear fruit. And the Spirit of the Lord *shall rest*

upon him, the Spirit of wisdom and understanding, the Spirit of counsel and might, the Spirit of knowledge and the fear of the LORD. And his delight shall be in the fear of the LORD." (Is. 11:1–3. See also Jer. 23:5, 33:15; Zech. 3:8, 6:12)

Here, the prophet Isaiah (one of the singing "men of old" in the carol) describes the coming Messiah as a blossoming branch coming from a "stump." He's talking about a family tree. The people of God had put their hopes in the covenant promises God made with King David, that the throne of David's kingdom would stand forever (2 Sam. 7:13). And yet, years, decades, and generations went by and no such throne was set up. Far from it, the line of David had nearly been lost entirely! It was as though someone took an axe to the family tree and whacked away—leaving not a grand and growing oak, but a lifeless "stump."

But from that seemingly useless and dead stump, the promise will still spring up. Jesus of Nazareth, "the son of David" (Mt. 1:1), was the proof that God was not yet done with David's line. His promises had not failed, though the people feared they had. It seemed to them that all hope was lost. The carol speaks of the dead of winter, the middle of the night—as though time had run out and darkness had prevailed. But that's precisely when this flower bloomed in Bethlehem! God often surprises us the most when we expect it the least. Do you feel like time has run out for God to act for you, and that all hope is lost? Take heart: even when the night seems half spent, God is still at work.

Pray: *O God, how great are Your promises to us! I thank You that not one word You have spoken has ever failed. Give me the faith to trust that Your good purposes will always be worked out, even when I can't imagine how. In Jesus's name I pray. Amen.*

Reflect:

Read Jeremiah 33:14–16.

- What promises of God do you find hardest to accept? Why?
- Think of, and thank God for, a time when He was faithful and gracious to you, even when you felt helpless and at a loss.

DECEMBER 4:

"O Little Town of Bethlehem"

O little town of Bethlehem, how still we see thee lie;
Above thy deep and dreamless sleep the silent stars go by;
Yet in thy dark streets shineth the everlasting Light;
The hopes and fears of all the years are met in thee tonight.

–"O Little Town of Bethlehem," Phillips Brooks

The first line of this carol is drawn from the prophet Micah:

"But you, O Bethlehem Ephrathah,
who are too little to be among the clans of Judah,
from you shall come forth for me
one who is to be ruler in Israel,
whose coming forth is from of old,
from ancient days." (Mich. 5:2)

God has big plans for this "little town": it will be the birthplace of Israel's future ruler. And not just any ruler, either. This is none other than the

Messiah. Did you notice how Micah asserts that the Messiah is eternal? At the same time as looking forward to Jesus's birth in Bethlehem, this Old Testament prophet describes the Messiah as "from of old, from ancient days." This ancient one will be born in Bethlehem! He is both the once and future King of Israel.

But why would God choose Bethlehem, an unimportant one-horse town, for such an incredible moment? In one sense, because He can. We might expect lights, cameras, and a red carpet to be rolled out when the Messiah comes. But God doesn't operate according to human wisdom, and He isn't bound by our expectations. The incarnation is one of the clearest examples of how God turns our assumptions inside out:

> *"God chose what is foolish in the world to shame the wise; God chose what is weak in the world to shame the strong; God chose what is low and despised in the world, even things that are not, to bring to nothing things that are, so that no human being might boast in the presence of God." (1 Cor. 1:27–29)*

This carol invites us to look upon Bethlehem and marvel at the upside-down wisdom of God. It imagines the birth of Christ taking place on any old Wednesday or Thursday night; the town lying quiet and still, the houses dark as most everyone is in bed. But with the eye of faith, we can see something far more marvelous: the object of all our hopes and the answer to all our fears has come in the baby boy born that night. If God could bring the Savior out of a pitiful place like this, then we have every reason to expect Him to use other seemingly mundane or unimpressive things, too. He can even have a use for people like you and me.

Pray: *Lord, You are wiser than our wisdom, but sometimes it is hard to see that or accept that. If Jesus came from a place* *like Bethlehem, help me to believe that You can work mightily through the weakest of people and situations. Amen.*

Reflect:

Read Micah 5:1–5a.

- What are some of the promises made in this passage about the Messiah? How were they fulfilled in Christ?
- How would our lives be different if we embraced the fact that God uses weak, small, and foolish things to accomplish His plans?

DECEMBER 5:

"Thou Key of David"

O come, Thou Key of David, come,
And open wide our heavenly home;
Make safe the way that leads on high,
And close the path to misery.
Rejoice! Rejoice!
Emmanuel shall come to thee, O Israel.

–"O Come, O Come Emmanuel," traditional

When I was in theological training, the church I served didn't own a building and so had to rent from a school in the mornings and a neighboring Lutheran church in the evenings. For some reason, we only had a single key to the Lutheran church, and for some reason, I was in charge of it. Maybe you can see where this is going. One fateful Lord's Day evening, I was heading to the church when I realized I had left the key at our apartment, and turning back to get it would add forty minutes to my journey. When I finally arrived, the faithful flock was huddled around the door, waiting to be let into church.

The kingdom of God has a door as well, and it also has a single key. Fortunately, the one who holds it is Jesus Christ, and He never forgets it. In this carol, Israel longs for the coming of the Messiah, called the "Key of David." The language comes from Isaiah 22, where God removes a faithless ruler from Israel and promises a better leader:

> *"And he shall be a father to the inhabitants of Jerusalem and to the house of Judah. And I will place on his shoulder the key of the house of David. He shall open, and none shall shut; and he shall shut, and none shall open." (Is. 22:21–22)*

The "key of the house of David" is, as the name suggests, the key that grants entrance into David's kingdom. God promised a coming ruler who would welcome in the faithful and keep out enemies. But Isaiah looked beyond the Jerusalem of his day to a New Jerusalem, a heavenly city. Who would be the one who could open the way into this eternal dwelling place? Jesus tells us in Revelation 3:7 that *He* is the one "who has the key of David"—He's the only one who can do it.

This carol takes the theme and gives it a slight twist—it does not call Jesus "the one who *has* the Key of David," but literally the one who *is* the Key of David: "O Come, Thou Key of David," we sing. This is spot on! We come to Jesus, not because of what He has, but because of who He is. It is faith in His person and work that "makes safe the way that leads on high." He is the key, *and* He is the door, and it is through Him alone that we can get into our heavenly home (Jn. 10:9, 14:6). No wonder the people longed for the coming of the Messiah, Emmanuel!

Pray: *Lord, I have learned something of what it means to belong to Your kingdom. I cannot get in unless Jesus, who has all power and authority, opens the way. Thank You that You* *have sent Him not simply to open the door, but to be the door. I know in Him I am safe, and it's in His name that I pray. Amen.*

Reflect:

Read John 14:1–11.

- How does this carol teach us about the reality that Jesus is more than just the way to salvation, but is salvation itself?
- Think of times where you have been interested in the gifts that come from Christ, and not the Giver Himself. What steps need to be taken for you to repent and follow more fully after Christ?

DECEMBER 6:

"Let All Mortal Flesh Keep Silence"

Let all mortal flesh keep silence,
And with fear and trembling stand;
Ponder nothing earthly-minded,
For with blessing in His hand
Christ our God to earth descendeth,
Our full homage to demand.

—"Let All Mortal Flesh Keep Silence," liturgy of St. James, adapted by Gerard Moultrie

It might seem a bit odd that we sing a song about being silent. The moment we have moved our lips to sing this carol, it would appear we have failed to keep it's opening command! But not really. To understand why, we should consider the two passages in the Bible that inspire the hymn. First, Habakkuk 2:20, "But the Lord is in his holy temple; let all the earth keep silence before him." Second, Zechariah 2:13, "Be silent, all flesh, before the Lord, for he has roused himself from his holy dwelling."

While using similar language, these passages have different contexts from one another—both of which are instructive for us. Habakkuk writes as a warning, calling the people to prepare for the arrival of the Messiah. In particular, that preparation must mean the removal of idolatry and sin from the lives of God's people—God demands our "full homage," after all. Silence, in this instance, means reverence and submission and humble obedience.

In Zechariah, the call to submissive silence is less a warning as it is a message of mouth-stopping, jaw-dropping hope. It comes in the context of his prophecy that God will dwell with His people:

> *"I will dwell in your midst, and you shall know that the LORD of hosts has sent me to you. And the LORD will inherit Judah as his portion in the holy land, and will again choose Jerusalem." (Zech. 2:11–12)*

This promise, given at a time when the exiled Israelites had returned to a country in ruins, was almost too good to be true. You see, it is not only that God would allow us to dwell with Him, as though He left open the door to heaven and said, "Come on in!" That would be amazing enough. But it's more than that: *He leaves* His holy dwelling and *comes to us.* As the carol puts it, "Christ our God to earth descendeth!"

What's your response to this? Zechariah is saying, "Be silent for a moment and sit with this thought: the God of heaven and earth, is moving from heaven to earth—not to *judge* you, not to *punish* you, but to *live with you!*" Once you've pondered this reality of heaven come down to earth in the person of Christ, you know what you will want to do? Sing!

Pray: *Lord, words fail me in offering thanks to You that You have not abandoned Your people, but have come down from* *heaven to make a new home with us forever. You are amazingly kind and hospitable, and I praise You in Jesus's name. Amen.*

Reflect:

Read Habakkuk 2:18–20.

- Why is stillness and silence so difficult for us?
- What are you anxious about? In what ways this very week do you need to practice reverential stillness and trust in God's work in your life?

DECEMBER 7:

"Risen with Healing in His Wings"

Hail the heaven-born Prince of Peace!
Hail the Sun of Righteousness!
Light and life to all He brings,
Risen with healing in His wings.

–"Hark! the Herald Angels Sing," Charles Wesley

Perhaps you didn't realize, but when you sing Charles Wesley's beloved words you are actually singing from the Minor Prophets! The past few days we have seen that the Old Testament Scriptures are full of predictions and prophecies about the arrival of the Savior: Genesis, Isaiah, Jeremiah, Micah, Habakkuk, and Zechariah have all been quoted in the carols we have considered thus far. Today we turn to Malachi:

> *"For behold, the day is coming, burning like an oven, when all the arrogant and all evildoers will be stubble. The day that is coming shall set them ablaze, says the* Lord *of hosts, so that it will leave them neither root nor branch.* ***But for you who fear my name, the***

> ***sun of righteousness shall rise with healing in its wings.***"
> *(Mal. 4:1–2, my emphasis)*

Malachi predicts a future day with two kinds of heat—one that hurts and one that heals. On that Last Day, all those who gave themselves over to evil shall receive the penalty due them for their sins. The Lord "shall set them ablaze." But for those who have placed their hope and trust in the Lord, "the sun of righteousness shall rise with healing in its wings." Here, Malachi looks forward, beyond the birth of the Savior, to the benefits we will receive from His rising and returning in glory.

"Wings" is another word for the rays of the sun. I write this while enduring a standard cold and dark Michigan winter. The light of the sun is so rare during these months that no matter how cold it is, my son and I make sure to run outside and bask in the rays if the sun ever peeks through the gloom. We call them our "sun breaks"—we stand outside, sometimes hopping up and down because it's literally freezing, but forcing ourselves to close our eyes and lift our heads to the sun for as long as we can. In God's design, the light of the sun has healing properties, and in the winter we feel our need for them!

Wesley is helpful in making clear that the sun bringing the most healing isn't the one up in the heavens, but rather "the heaven-born Prince of Peace," the Son of God. The dark of December is a good time for us to remember what we need to be doing all the year round: looking to Jesus Christ as our only help and hope from the downward drag of sin. The nineteenth-century Scottish minister Robert Murray McCheyne gave great advice: "For every look at yourself, take ten looks at Christ." That is what it means to "hail the Sun of Righteousness": to behold Him by faith in all His beauty, and soak in the life that He gives.

Pray: *Father, cause me to look to the "Righteous Sun." In His light alone do I see light, and in His life do I have mine. Amen.*

Reflect:

Read Malachi 4.

- What is the significance of biblical imagery calling God a "sun"? Do you think of Him in this way?
- In what ways does the resurrection of Christ "heal" us?

DECEMBER 8:

"Tell Out, My Soul, the Greatness of the Lord"

Tell out, my soul, the greatness of the Lord!
Unnumbered blessings give my spirit voice;
Tender to me the promise of His Word;
In God my Savior shall my heart rejoice.

–"Tell Out, My Soul," Timothy Dudley-Smith[1]

The time has finally come—all of those prophecies from of old are about to be fulfilled! It begins with a humble and obscure young girl from Nazareth we simply know as Mary. It's hard for us to imagine just how bizarre and terrifying the angel's visit must have been for her. Not only will she, a virgin, conceive a child (as if that wasn't crazy enough!), but the child in question "will be great and will be called the Son of the Most High. And the Lord God will give to him the throne of his father David, and he will reign over the house of

1 Words: Timothy Dudley-Smith © 1962, Ren. 1990 Hope Publishing Company, www.hopepublishing.com. All rights reserved. Used by permission.

Jacob forever, and of his kingdom there will be no end" (Lk. 1:32–33). It is too astounding to take in, and yet Mary's response is filled with faith: "I am the servant of the Lord, let it be to me according to your word" (v. 39).

Shortly after, while visiting her cousin Elizabeth, Mary expands upon her reaction to this sudden turn of events in song. Hers is the very first Christmas carol, followed swiftly by three others in Luke, and is often referred to as the Magnificat.[2] It is a song that is bursting forth with praise from beginning to end, with not even a hint of fear or uncertainty.

Despite not being traditionally associated with Christmas, "Tell Out, My Soul" is worthy of any advent carol service. The Anglican Bishop Timothy Dudley-Smith has captured the heart of Mary's song as she anticipates the birth of the Savior in such a way as to make it fitting for every believer to sing. We, like Mary, ought to respond to God's promises by loving them and cherishing them—"Tender to me the promise of His Word!" Instead of doubt and suspicion, we should respond with rejoicing that the sovereign Lord of the universe uses His power to shower upon us "unnumbered blessings"—the greatest of which is His Son sent to save us from our sins. Does that sound too good to be true? Learn from Mary. She greets the seemingly impossible with an amazing song of faith, because she knew what we so often forget: "with God all things are possible" (Mt. 19:26).

Pray: *Gracious Father, I thank You that You make amazing promises to me in Your Word, and that with You, nothing is too good to be true. In Jesus's name I pray. Amen.*

2 This title comes from the Latin for the first line in verse 46, "My soul *magnifies*…"

Reflect:

Read Luke 1:46–56.

- What is a major theme(s) in Mary's song? How can we incorporate her perspective into our prayer life?
- Reflect on a time in your life when God proved to you that with Him all things are possible.

DECEMBER 9:

"Begotten, not Created"

God of God, Light of Light;
Lo, He abhors not the virgin's womb;
Very God, begotten not created;
O come, let us adore Him, Christ the Lord.

–"O Come, All Ye Faithful," Adeste Fideles,
translation by Frederick Oakeley

The best Christian hymns will teach you good theology. This is especially true in "O Come, All Ye Faithful," where the second verse quotes almost directly from the ancient Nicene Creed:

"We believe … in one Lord Jesus Christ, the only-begotten Son of God, begotten of his Father before all worlds, God of God, Light of Light, very God of very God, begotten, not made, being of one substance with the Father … "

We sing the carol quite effortlessly each Christmas season, and yet we are indebted to the arduous labors of our church fathers for these words, as they fought bravely to protect the church from heresy.

Allow me a brief historical aside. In AD 325, the Emperor Constantine summoned all the church's bishops to meet in the city of Nicaea (modern-day Iznik, Turkey), and well over two hundred gathered to hammer out some disagreements. A man named Arius was causing a major problem by teaching that Christ was the first created being, rather than the eternal Son of God. His slogan was "There was a time when He [Jesus] was not." The Council of Nicaea rejected this claim by insisting, as the Bible does, that Jesus is as much God as the Father. All the perfections ("light") in God are in Christ as well—they share the same holiness, knowledge, power, wisdom—everything! And since Christ was eternally "begotten, not created," Arius' slogan now had a new rejoinder: "There was not when He was not."

And incredibly, marvelously, mysteriously, the Second Person of the Trinity, being fully God, was willing also to become fully man: "Lo, He abhors not the virgin's womb." The one true God became one of us. He did not despise this mission, nor disdain this responsibility. In biblical language, "he is not ashamed to call [us] brothers" (Heb. 2:11).

Pray: *Thank You for revealing that Christ is both God and man, and for the creeds and hymns that have helped the Christian church remember these truths. Let me never fail to adore Christ as my Lord! Amen.*

Reflect:

Read Colossians 1:15–19.

- What are some biblical proofs that Jesus is really "God of God"?
- The Bible tells us that Jesus has the fullness of deity within Him, but also that He is not ashamed to be made like us, His brothers

and sisters, in every respect. What is the proper response to these profound truths?

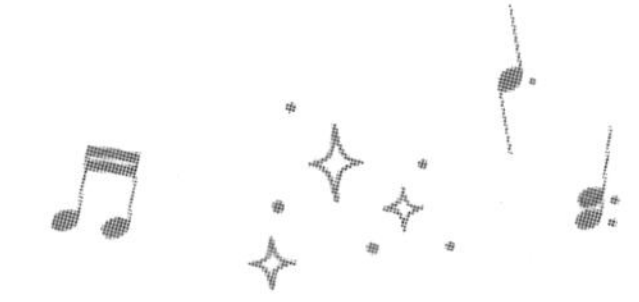

DECEMBER 10:

"Word of the Father"

Yea, Lord we greet Thee, born this happy morning,
Jesus to Thee be all glory given;
Word of the Father, now in flesh appearing!
O come, let us adore Him, Christ the Lord!

–"O Come, All Ye Faithful," translation by Frederick Oakeley

In the Bible, there's a lot packed into the little word "Word." It's how John kicks off his gospel account on the life of Christ: "In the beginning was the Word, and the Word was with God, and the Word was God" (Jn. 1:1). That's a peculiar way to speak about Jesus. What does John mean? The Greek term used here is *logos*. A profound concept in the ancient world, the *logos* was the "logic" or truth or reason which held everything together. It was the power that made sense of the world.

John's original audience wouldn't have been all that surprised to hear that "In the beginning there was the *Logos*." "Of course that's right," they would have thought. The Word, Logic, transcends time and reality. And John is equating this Logic with God Himself. God is the eternal principle that makes sense of the world. So far, so good. But then John really does surprise his readers: this Logic is not just a principle, but a person! "And the Word was made flesh, and dwelt among us" (v. 14, KJV).

This is the most succinct statement on the incarnation you will ever find. John puts it briefly and bluntly. He does not say that the Word looked like a man, or was human-like, but that He became that most basic aspect of our humanity: *flesh*. He didn't just look like us. He became us, made up of the very same fibers as you and me.

Further, He lived among us. His home was heaven and yet willingly, voluntarily, joyfully He made His home on earth. He who was from all eternity God, becomes man, and will remain both God and man for the rest of all eternity. It is hard to surpass the words of an old catechism here:

> *"... the Lord Jesus Christ ... being the eternal Son of God, became man, and so was, and continues to be, God and man in two distinct natures, and one person, forever."*[1]

What a Savior!

Pray: *Dear Jesus, You are above and beyond us in every way. You were at the beginning and before the beginning. By You all things were made. But You were also made flesh, to redeem us from sin. Jesus, to You be all glory given, from now on and for all eternity! Amen.*

1 Westminster Shorter Catechism, Question and Answer 21.

Reflect:

Read John 1:1–14.

- What is the significance of John speaking of Jesus as "the Word"?
- Jesus did not become human for a short stint while here on earth, but will bear our human nature for all of eternity. Why does this comfort the Christian?

DECEMBER 11:

"Priest in the Manger"

Priest in the manger, who now sympathizes,
Wearing our nature and clothed in disgrace.
O what a myst'ry that every saint prizes:
Why would this Priest come and die in our place?

–"In the Manger," Jonathan Landry Cruse[1]

The past few days we have been considering the mystery of the incarnation—God become flesh (see 1 Tim. 3:16). How is it that the divine is able to put on humanity, and be both fully God and fully man? Christians have understood that although we cannot ever comprehend *how* this happened, we must affirm *that* it happened.

But the mystery runs even deeper, for the gospel reveals not only that God was born, but also that He died. In fact, He was born for this very purpose. He *became* man to die *as* man *for* man. In the manger lies our Priest—our representative before God—who "appeared once

1 This is a new carol. You can find the full score in the appendix, or download it free and hear a recording, at www.hymnsofdevotion.com/in-the-manger

for all at the end of the ages to put away sin by the sacrifice of himself" (Heb. 9:26). This is the real mystery, is it not? It's not just the question of *how*, but the question of *why*: "Why would this Priest come and die in our place?" Again, we cannot fully know the reasons why Christ came and died for us, but we must affirm that He did. It is a mystery "that every saint prizes," in the words of this carol. The mystery is reason for praise:

> *"Oh, the depth of the riches and wisdom and knowledge of God! How unsearchable are his judgments and how inscrutable his ways! ... For from him and through him and to him are all things. To him be glory forever. Amen." (Rom. 11:33, 36)*

Many centuries ago, St. Augustine made this staggering observation about the incarnation. May it expand your appreciation and enlarge your praise for the incarnation this Christmas:

> *"Man's maker was made man that He, Ruler of the stars, might nurse at His mother's breast; that the Bread might hunger, the Fountain thirst, the Light sleep, the Way be tired on its journey; that Truth might be accused of false witnesses, the Teacher be beaten with whips, the Foundation be suspended on wood; that Strength might grow weak; that the Healer might be wounded; that Life might die."*

Pray: *Almighty God, I cannot fully understand how Christ came for me, or why, but I believe that He did. Thank You that You have sent a Priest to die in my place, so may I now live for Him. Amen.*

Reflect:

Read Hebrews 2:17–18.

- Priests in the Old Covenant made continual sacrifices for sin. How does this differ from the way in which Jesus is our priest?
- The incarnation is a mystery, to be sure. So is the crucifixion. What sort of response do such mysteries call for?

DECEMBER 12:

"Angels We Have Heard on High"

Angels we have heard on high,
Sweetly singing o'er the plains,
And the mountains in reply
Echoing their joyous strains:
Gloria in excelsis Deo.

–"Angels We Have Heard on High," traditional

In the opening of the book of Hebrews, the author writes to a group of Christians who were particularly taken with angels. He wants to prove that however glorious and wonderful angels may be (and they are!), Jesus is far more glorious and far more wonderful. He quotes from Psalm 97 to say that one of the ways we know that Jesus is truly the Son of God is that when He comes into the world angels will worship Him: "When he brings the firstborn into the world, he says, 'Let all God's angels worship him'" (Heb. 1:6).

Sure enough, some two thousand years ago the night sky in Bethlehem was filled with the evidence that the baby boy born there was much more than met the eye:

> *"And suddenly there was with the angel a multitude of the heavenly host praising God and saying, 'Glory to God in the highest, and on earth peace among those with whom he is pleased!'"* (Lk. 2:13–14)

The people receiving the letter of Hebrews might have been infatuated with angels, but the angels were, and are, infatuated with Jesus.

Are you? Do you admire Jesus in the way that even the sinless angels in heaven do? Do you lend your voice to the song of the angels, singing, "Glory to God in the highest!"? (That's what the Latin phrase "*Gloria in excelsis Deo*" means that we sing in this carol.) Do you want to spend your waking moments in intentional praise and exultation of Christ—in your thoughts, affections, speech, and song? We have more reason to worship Christ than the angels, after all. They have never sinned nor needed a Savior. He means so much more to us! Since we have Christ, since we have His atoning blood, since we have His love, then He should have our song. Worship is the outward expression that our very hearts belong to someone or something. Does your heart belong to Jesus? If it does, worship should and will flow from you.

Pray: *My desire is that all creation–myself included!–would join in praising You, O Triune God of glory. You are so good to me, especially in sending Your Son to live and die for me. Let me always praise You for it. I pray it in Christ's name. Amen.*

Reflect:

Read Hebrews 1:5–14.

- How is the angelic response to the birth of Christ instructive for our own response?
- Think of this: your songs of praise to God are more beautiful in His ear than the songs of angels. Why?

DECEMBER 13:

"Christ the Babe Was Born for You!"

Flocks were sleeping, shepherds keeping
Vigil till the morning new
Saw the glory, heard the story,
Tidings of a gospel true.
Thus rejoicing, free from sorrow,
Praises voicing, greet the morrow:
Christ the babe was born for you!

–"Infant Holy, Infant Lowly," Piotrowi Skadze, paraphrased by Edith M. G. Reed

The announcement from the angelic chorus to the shepherds was personal. "For unto *you* is born this day..." (Lk. 2:11, emphasis mine). How could that be? Shepherds were near peasants, one of the lowest social classes at the time. From a Jewish perspective they also were disadvantaged, as being surrounded constantly by dirty animals made them ceremonially unclean. Could it really be that the Savior, Christ the Lord, is for them? Yes! And the sign to prove it was they would find Him lying in a manger (v. 12). Imagine the joy that overcame them as they rushed to Bethlehem, and behold, there He was, sleeping in a feeding trough of all places! Surrounded by dirty animals, just like them! This Savior was born into the filth that defined them as a despised class of citizens. Truly, He was born for *them*.

He is born for you and me as well. Long before the angel announced it to the shepherds, Isaiah announced it to God's people: "For to *us* a child is born, to *us* a son is given" (Is. 9:6, emphasis mine). He is the one to deliver us! Jesus, anointed and appointed by the Spirit to take care of our sin problem, is God's greatest gift *for* us. How do we know? Because He came as one of us. Hebrews 2:17 says He was made like His brothers in every respect. He shares our flesh and blood! He was born to know our every earthly grief, yet without sin so that He could be our substitute.

Is He yours? When my four-year-old son was learning this carol for a church program, the last line struck him as off. "Daddy, it should be 'Christ the babe is born for *us*,' not just *you*," he said, pointing at me. That's right! Christ came for every type of person and was born to save *all* who would trust in Him! But the knowledge that Christ came to save sinners doesn't do you any good unless you can first say, by faith, He came to save *me*.

Pray: *O God, I do not deserve the gift of Your Son. But I do believe that Christ was born for me, and that He loved me and gave Himself for me. Thank You for this indescribable gift! Amen.*

Reflect:

Read John 10:7–18.

- In what ways does God identify with you in Jesus Christ?

- What's the difference between saying "Christ died for His people" and "Christ died for me"? Can you say Christ died for you? Why or why not?

DECEMBER 14:

"A Manger Choosing for Your Throne"

All praise to You, eternal Lord,
Clothed in our human flesh and blood,
A manger choosing for your throne,
While worlds on worlds are yours alone.

–"All Praise to You," Martin Luther

The shepherds saw the newborn King—lying on a bed of straw. What do we make of that? It's so very important to understand that in leaving heaven, Christ didn't leave His kingship. Sometimes we speak of Christ "leaving" His throne (we even sing it in another popular carol, "Thou Didst Leave Thy Throne and Thy Kingly Crown"), and maybe we get the idea that at the incarnation Christ became something less than He was previously.

Rather than speaking of leaving a throne, it would be better to speak of exchanging a throne. Martin Luther expresses it well in this carol: Jesus *chose* that the manger should become His throne. Even as He lies upon a bed of straw, He is still ruling and reigning. He is still Lord. The world is still His. The incarnation is not about what He *loses*, it's about what He *chooses*. He chooses obscurity, poverty, a manger—but He loses nothing of His kingly deity.

That sort of upside-down kingship marked His birth as well as His death. The Eastern kings were looking for the one born king of the Jews (Mt. 2:2), and that's precisely the charge that got Him killed (Mt. 27:37). When He is finally acknowledged as "King of the Jews," it's in derision not praise (Mt. 27:29). He is then lifted up, not on a throne, but a cross. He is given not gold, but thorns, for a crown.

Just as at His birth, no one forces this upon the Son of God. He chooses this path. "No one takes [my life] from me, but I lay it down of my own accord" (Jn. 10:18). Why would He make such a choice? To deal with sin. To put away wickedness forever. To make sure that His forever kingdom is one of peace. He does it for us. As Luther goes on to write in this carol:

"You came to us in the darkest night
To make us children of the light,
To make us, in the realms divine,
As your own angels round You shine."

Pray: *Dear Jesus, I thank You that You would willingly leave Your rightful place in the heavens and come to earth, reigning as King in places like a cattle stall and on a cross. You are always and forever the Great King, and I love You. Amen.*

Reflect:

Read Matthew 27:27–31.

- In his time on earth, Jesus never once sat upon a kingly throne. Does that mean He was not reigning over all things?

- When Jesus was finally hailed "king of the Jews" it was on the cross. What does this teach us about the nature of His kingship? Is there a similar lesson taught at the incarnation?

DECEMBER 15:

"What Child Is This?"

What Child is this, who, laid to rest,
On Mary's lap is sleeping?
Whom angels greet with anthems sweet,
While shepherds watch are keeping?
This, this is Christ, the King,
Whom shepherds guard and angels sing:
Haste, haste to bring Him laud,
The Babe, the Son of Mary!

–"What Child Is This," traditional, adapted by William C. Dix

We are faced with countless questions every day: what to wear, what to eat, what route to take to work, what to do with the kids later, what to watch… These dilemmas are generally of little significance—choosing your outfit each morning is unlikely to be a matter of life or death! But greater decisions come as well: How will I vote? Whom will I marry? Even so, these pale in comparison to the most important question we could ever answer. It's the question Jesus posed to Peter: "Who do you say that I am?" (Mk. 8:29).

Christmas provides us with a good time to reflect on this. Everywhere we see the lights, the gifts, the decorations, all the food, but as we look beyond all the commercialism we do well to ask, Why is it that millions of people around the world celebrate the birth of this one boy? Why is our entire calendar based on the date of His arrival? Look back even further: Why would the angelic hosts of heaven and a lowly band of shepherds alike worship the arrival of this particular individual? If Jesus isn't Savior and Lord, then we are left asking—with no satisfying answer—what *is* the big deal? There shouldn't be a big deal at all!

So—who is Jesus? Your eternal destiny hangs or falls on how you answer that one simple question. Maybe you have sung this carol hundreds of times but never really asked yourself the question: "What child *is* this, after all?" It would be hard to improve upon the answer this song provides: "This, this is Christ, the King."

Pray: *Lord, reveal to me more and more the reality of who Christ is, that I would have courage to say, Jesus is my Savior and King! It is through His person and perfection that I come to You now in prayer. Amen.*

Reflect:

Read Matthew 16:13–16.

- If someone asked you, "Who is Jesus?" what answer would you give?
- Why is this such an important question?

DECEMBER 16:

"Go, Tell It!"

Go, tell it on the mountain, over the hills and everywhere;
Go, tell it on the mountain that Jesus Christ is born.

–"Go Tell It on the Mountain," African American spiritual

After the shepherds encountered the newborn Christ, we are told that "they spread the word concerning what had been told them about this child" (Lk. 2:17, NIV). The birth of the Messiah, the long-awaited answer to all of mankind's troubles, was truly *gospel*, truly good news. And good news *needs* to be shared. The shepherds understood that. This beloved song tells their story—"while shepherds kept their watching o'er silent flocks by night, behold, throughout the heavens there shone a holy light"—but then turns to us, as it were, and implores us to follow their example of spreading the word of Jesus's birth.

People who believe do so because someone, at some point or another, told them about Jesus. Have you ever thought about that? If you are a Christian, it is because you were told about the Christian message. Maybe from your parents, your co-workers, your friends, your neighbors, your pastor, or your Sunday school teachers. Paul writes in Romans 10 that this is God's pattern for salvation: 1) the gospel is shared, 2) the gospel is heard, 3) the gospel is believed.

> *"How then will they call on him in whom they have not believed? And how are they to believe in him of whom they have never heard? And how are they to hear without someone preaching? And how are they to preach unless they are sent? As it is written, 'How beautiful are the feet of those who preach the good news!' ... So faith comes from hearing, and hearing through the word of Christ." (Rom. 10:14–15, 17)*

God could very well use your words about the gospel to a friend or family member as the means of bringing them to salvation. Since that is the case, we have every reason to go and tell it everywhere, and to everyone, that Jesus Christ is born!

Pray: *Lord, I thank You that I have heard the greatest news in the world–that Jesus Christ was born to save me from my sins. Let me be quick to share it with others. Amen.*

Reflect:

Read Matthew 28:16–20.

- It can be hard to share the truth about Jesus and the gospel. Why? What sorts of thoughts and fears keep us from telling others the good news?
- The best way to prepare for evangelism is through prayer. Think of one or two people you could pray for, asking that the Lord would give you an opportunity to tell them about Jesus and share the good news.

DECEMBER 17:

"Joyful Steps"

As with joyful steps they sped
To that lowly cradle-bed,
There to bend the knee before
Him whom heaven and earth adore;
So may we with willing feet
Ever seek Thy mercy seat.

–"As with Gladness Men of Old," William C. Dix

We often drag our feet in spiritual matters. Maybe we don't outright despise church or prayer or family worship, but we do not prioritize them either. We will "get around" to them when we have the time, we tell ourselves. We'll make them a priority … next week. Our hearts are often infected with spiritual apathy.

But the more real God becomes to us, the more we will want to be with Him. That was the experience of the wise men from the East. They could not shake this calling that the Great King had arrived, and so they journeyed far to find Him. The closer they got, the happier they became:

"When they saw the star, they rejoiced exceedingly with great joy. And going into the house, they saw the child with Mary his mother, and they fell down and worshiped him. Then, opening their treasures, they offered him gifts, gold and frankincense and myrrh." (Mt. 2:10–11)

William C. Dix captures their mood in his carol, saying these men of old beheld the star with "gladness," and "with joyful steps they sped" to find the Savior.

Do "joyful steps" describe how you follow after God? If not, this stanza offers a good prayer to make your own. It helps us to ask, "Lord, let me never be slow to come to You! Let me be quick to find You in prayer and worship!" Once you have beheld the glory of God in Jesus Christ, you will want nothing less than to keep beholding it. The pleasures of this world will fade away and you will not be so prone to run after them. Let the love of Christ redirect your life entirely this Christmas. It may mean giving up old loves and passions and hobbies, yes. But it will mean immense blessings, too. You won't be disappointed.

Pray: *Lord, forgive me for the times I joylessly drag my feet to meet with You. Make me be quick to obey You and eager to follow after You, for Jesus's sake. Amen.*

Reflect:

Read Mark 8:34.

- Why can we be so lethargic in our spiritual life? How can you capture the joy of the wise men in your life?
- What sorts of practices or habits do you need to put in place in your life to follow after Jesus more closely?

DECEMBER 18:

"What Can I Give Him?"

What can I give Him, poor as I am?
If I were a shepherd I would bring a lamb,
If I were a wise man I would do my part
But what I can I give Him–give my heart.

–"In the Bleak Midwinter," Christina Rossetti

The wise men were not only prompt in coming to Jesus, they were prepared. They brought gifts fitting the grand occasion of meeting a king: "Then, opening their treasures, they offered him gifts, gold and frankincense and myrrh" (Mt. 2:11). Some have tried to uncover a theological meaning embedded within each of the three gifts that were presented, and there may be something to that, though we wouldn't want to stress it too much. For example, I think it unlikely that myrrh was given to the baby Jesus as an intentional omen of His coming death, even though we are able to look back now and make the connection (Mk. 15:23). The point is simply that the wise men brought the very best gifts that they could.

The story of the wise men's gifts has been co-opted by our culture to prove that Christmas is a time for gift-giving. I'll be the first to admit, I'm a fan of getting gifts at Christmas! But notice that the Eastern kings do not give gifts to one another, but to Jesus. That's the gift that matters most at Christmastime: the one we are going to give in honor of the King.

But what could that possibly be? In her great Christmas poem, Christina Rossetti wrestles with the plain fact that nothing we have could be a tribute fitting enough, or a gift worthy enough, for *this* King. He is too grand and glorious and good. But in her concluding line she lands upon the only right answer: "give my heart." This is the only gift that makes sense for Jesus. After all, it's not one thing, it's everything. All that we are and have we consecrate to Him. Jesus told us this is what He wants from us when He said, "whoever loses his life for my sake will find it" (Mt. 10:39).

Pray: *Lord Jesus, I offer my heart to You promptly and sincerely. Amen.*

Reflect:

Read Psalm 116:12–14.

- Christmas is inseparable from gift-giving. In what ways can this be helpful and in what ways can it be harmful in terms of our conception of the true meaning of Christmas? What's the most important gift you could give Jesus?
- Today our prayer was that we be enabled to give our hearts to God "promptly and sincerely." What would that look like for you?

DECEMBER 19:

"Thy Holy Face"

Silent night! Holy night!
Son of God, love's pure light
Radiant beams from thy holy face
With the dawn of redeeming grace,
Jesus, Lord, at Thy birth!

–"Silent Night," Joseph Mohr

This verse contains one of those instances where poetry gets slightly unhitched from reality. Go to any maternity ward and you will learn it is anything but silent! Beyond that, Joseph Mohr pictures the newborn Jesus as having God's pure love beaming radiantly from His face. Many paintings of the manger scene likewise include a glimmer about the Christ child, or perhaps a spotlight coming down from the heavens, or a halo shining above His and His mother's heads. But Jesus was fully human—and human faces don't have beams of light bursting from them. If they did that would be quite terrifying!

I write this only three days after the birth of my third child, Caleb.

His face is the most adorable thing I have ever seen. But that's because he's a baby, not because he is divine. If people were to remark upon the newborn in Bethlehem it would have been to say something like, "Aw, how cute!" Or, "Look how He has His mother's nose!" Not, "Look at those light beams shining from His eyes!"

As a human, Jesus's face was completely normal. And yet, the carol is absolutely right to say His face was also "holy." Everything about Jesus was holy. To redeem us from sin He needed to be our substitute—like us in every way, "yet without sin" (Heb. 4:15). And such is the infiltrating effects of sin—it so corrupts every part of our being—that we easily forget it's actually *unnatural* to us. Being human does not equal being sinful. God made mankind upright (Eccl. 7:29); Adam and Eve were without sin.

But Jesus is the only baby ever to be born without sin. He is the only one of whom it could be said, "therefore the child to be born will be called holy" (Lk. 1:35). That stupendous fact makes us feel we need to capture the event with halos and "radiant beams"—but that's not necessary. Mary held in her arms the type of person we were all meant to be: a fully human yet entirely sinless child. Thanks to the arrival of this Holy One, who gives us His holiness and takes our sin, we too will be sinless one day soon. And because that future is so certain, even now we can be called "saints," or "holy ones" (1 Cor. 1:2).

Pray: *Dear Lord, thank You for sending Your own Son, like us in every way but without sin. Thank You that, because He has died in our place, You have declared an end to sin's control over us. Thank You that the righteous requirement of the law has been fulfilled and there is now no condemnation for those of us who belong to Jesus. Help us to live lives shaped by the Holy Spirit! Amen.*

Reflect:

Read 1 Peter 2:22.

- Why are we tempted to conjure up images of the Christ-child with halos and other non-human-like features? Why is this dangerous for our perception of Jesus?
- Why is the holiness of Christ critical for the Christian?

DECEMBER 20:

"All for Love's Sake"

Thou who wast rich beyond all splendor,
All for love's sake becamest poor;
Thrones for a manger did surrender,
Sapphire-paved courts for stable floor.

–"Thou Who Wast Rich beyond All Splendor,"
Frank Houghton

It is impossible to remove love from God's purpose in salvation. It stands at the very center of God's plan to redeem a people for Himself. The goal is His glory (Eph. 1:6), but the motivation is love (Eph. 1:4–5). Love is who God is (1 Jn. 4:8), to such an extent that it overflows from Him. He is "*abounding* in steadfast love," (Ex. 34:6, emphasis mine) and we experience it in the gift of His Son: "For God so *loved* the world, that he gave his only begotten Son" (Jn. 3:16 KJV, emphasis mine).

The Son joins the Father in this full and free love. In fact, John says that if you want to define and discern God's love, you have to look to the Son: "By this we know love, that he laid down his life for us"

(1 Jn. 3:16). Much of our anxiety and spiritual doubts would be cured if we would consistently bathe our souls in this truth: it was "all for love's sake" that Christ came from heaven, became poor, was born in a manger, and even died upon a cross. It was not because we deserved it, not because we earned it, not because we checked some boxes, not because we met any criteria whatsoever. It was *all* for love's sake. The pressure is off.

What is your response to this love? It needs to be twofold. The first response is to *accept it*. No one can benefit from any gift unless they first receive it and open it. This is the most difficult part of Christianity for some people: believing that it's actually for them. But you must. Can you share Paul's testimony, that "the Son of God ... loved me and gave himself for me" (Gal. 2:20)?

Once you accept God's gift of love, the second response is to *return it*. Not like we do at the department stores immediately following the holidays with our gift receipts. We give love back to God in gratitude and happy obedience. Christ was willing to exchange the throne of heaven for a pitiful manger on earth, all for love's sake. Now, all for love's sake, we must be ready to surrender self and sin for Him. He more than deserves it.

Pray: *Father, thank You for lavishing Your love upon me—freely and without compulsion. Thank You, O Son, that all for love's sake You would leave the riches of heaven for the poverty of earth. Now, O Spirit, produce that same selfless love in my heart, that I may serve You, the Triune God, all my days. Amen.*

Reflect:

Read 2 Corinthians 8:9.

- What are some Bible passages, beyond those given in the devotional today, which speak of God's love for us?
- In what ways can you "return" God's gift of love today?

DECEMBER 21:

"Born to Give Them Second Birth"

Mild, He lays His glory by,
Born that man no more may die,
Born to raise the sons of earth,
Born to give them second birth.

–"Hark! The Herald Angels Sing," Charles Wesley

Many eager and well-meaning evangelists have puzzled people with the startling question, "Are you born again?!" The phrase is common in Christian-talk, but on the face of it makes no sense. Remember how it confused poor Nicodemus:

> *"Jesus answered him, 'Truly, truly, I say to you, unless one is born again he cannot see the kingdom of God.' Nicodemus said to him, 'How can a man be born when he is old? Can he enter a second time into his mother's womb and be born?'" (Jn. 3:3–4)*

Jesus was teaching on the necessity of the "second birth"—or "regeneration"

—without which no one can enter into eternity. The idea is that we need to be brought to life. The Bible says that we are "dead in our trespasses" but God "made us alive together with Christ" (Eph. 2:5). Because Christ was born on earth, lived a perfect life, died, but now lives again, we can be made alive as well. He was born to bring us true life. The earthly birth of Christ has everything to do with our heavenly birth. And having a heavenly birth secures us from a hellish death.

Did you know that, according to Scripture, there are two types of birth *and* two types of death? The first birth is our natural entrance into the world; the second birth is becoming a Christian. The first death is our natural exit from this world; the second death is eternal judgment. But the promise of God is that those who have a second birth, will never need to taste the second death. For those who share in the life of Christ—born again of His Spirit in this life and guaranteed resurrection in the next—"the second death has no power" (Rev. 20:6).

The formula goes like this: those who are born only once must die twice, but those who are born twice will only die once. As Charles Wesley teaches us in this carol, Christ was born to give us "second birth," and ensure that we "no more may die." Praise Him!

Pray: *Lord Jesus, thank You for being born in this world, so that I could experience a new birth that brings me into the next. Amen.*

Reflect:

Read Titus 3:4–7.

- How would you describe what "regeneration" is to someone who asked you?
- Regeneration means new birth, and it brings about an entirely new life for us. What are some ways you have experienced that newness, or ways you want to experience newness in your life?

DECEMBER 22:

"To Save Us All from Satan's Power"

God rest you merry, gentlemen, let nothing you dismay;
Remember Christ our Savior was born on Christmas Day
To save us all from Satan's power when we were gone astray.
O tidings of comfort and joy, comfort and joy;
O tidings of comfort and joy!

–"God Rest Ye Merry, Gentlemen," traditional

This carol shows its age. "Rest you merry" is not a phrase we use anymore, though it was more common in sixteenth- and seventeenth-century English. "Merry" is not a description of jolly gentlemen, rather, it refers to the state of peace and happiness. And "rest" isn't about sitting down with a coffee but a verb meaning "to keep." If we updated the language, the opening line would go something like, "May God keep you all in perfect tranquility and contentment."

To this end, the carol says we need to remember something: that Jesus Christ was born to put an end to Satan and his dominion. We often reflect on the birth of Christ as something quaint and picturesque, maybe like a scene out of a Thomas Kinkade painting. Each Christmas, many of us set out cute figurines reenacting the nativity: reverent Mary, proud Joseph, dignified wise men, singing angels, kneeling shepherds, and, of course, lowing oxen. But Revelation teaches that there is another character present who is often missing from our mantlepieces: Satan. Revelation gives us the vivid image of the devil's desire to defeat the Savior: "And the dragon stood before the woman who was about to give birth, so that when she bore her child he might devour it" (Rev. 12:4). But Satan's plans were frustrated and, instead, the birth of Christ was the beginning of the end of the conflict between heaven and hell. Jesus was born to put the devil to death. The crying babe in the cattle trough is the mighty Champion who comes to crush the serpent (Gen. 3:15). He comes to "save us all from Satan's power."

To the extent we forget that Jesus has overcome the devil, our internal peace will slip. The wiles of Satan in the world will seem to win. We'll become scared and lose confidence in our salvation. As the great Accuser, he will drudge up our past sins and bring us to despair, doubting the truth of God's offer of reconciliation. But lasting comfort and joy comes when we embrace this truth: "The reason the Son of God appeared was to destroy the works of the devil" (1 Jn. 3:8).

Pray: *Father in heaven, thank You that You do not allow Satan to have sway over Your people. Thank You for sending Christ to save us from his power, and may this give us lasting peace. In His name I pray. Amen.*

Reflect:

Read Revelation 12.

- Do you ever feel like Satan is assailing you? When are you most prone to feel tempted or discouraged by him?

- How does Satan try to trick us now into thinking that he hasn't already been crushed by Christ? What should you do in those moments?

DECEMBER 23:

"Thou Long-Expected Jesus"

Come, Thou long-expected Jesus,
Born to set Thy people free;
From our fears and sins release us,
Let us find our rest in Thee.
Israel's Strength and Consolation,
Hope of all the earth Thou art;
Dear Desire of every nation,
Joy of every longing heart.

–"Come, Thou Long-Expected Jesus,"
Charles Wesley

The opening line of this carol is a bit of an understatement. "Long-expected" doesn't even begin to express the waiting and anticipation that the people of God had for their Messiah. The problem in Jesus's day, however, was that God's people had been waiting so long that when He finally arrived many refused to believe it:

> *"Coming to his hometown he taught them in their synagogue, so that they were astonished, and said, 'Where did this man get this wisdom and these mighty works? Is not this the carpenter's son?' … And they took offense at him." (Mt. 13:54–55, 57)*

Imagine an engaged couple who have spent the past six months apart from each other. At long last, they are to be reunited. The man anxiously waits at the airport for his fiancée to step out of the gate. Now, what would you think if, upon seeing her, he turned up his nose and said, "Actually, you're not what I want anymore, after all." Let's say he then slapped her, turned his back, and walked away. We would be appalled. Here is the person who is supposed to love her the most totally rejecting and humiliating her! And yet, that's precisely what the majority of Israel did to Jesus upon His long-awaited arrival. As it turns out, even though they were expecting a Messiah, Jesus wasn't the Messiah they were expecting.

The fascinating character Simeon stands out as a contrast. He knew Jesus to be "Israel's Strength and Consolation"—a phrase that Wesley borrows from Simeon's story. Simeon "was righteous and devout, waiting for the consolation of Israel" (Lk. 2:25) and God rewards this saint's faith by permitting him to see—and hold—the Savior he had been long-expecting. "He took him up in his arms and blessed God and said, 'Lord, now you are letting your servant depart in peace'" (vv. 28–29). All those who find their rest in Jesus now, who claim Him to be the joy of their longing hearts, who acknowledge Him to be the One who is exactly what they need, will be granted the same reward as Simeon: seeing Jesus face to face.

Pray: *Lord, give me the faith I need to rest in Jesus, trusting that He is the answer to my every need. As Israel once awaited His arrival, I now await His return when I will get to see my Savior. Keep me faithful until the end. Amen.*

Reflect:

Read Luke 12:35–40.

- Would you say Jesus is your "strength and consolation"? Why or why not?
- How can you remind yourself, and others, that waiting for Jesus is worth it?

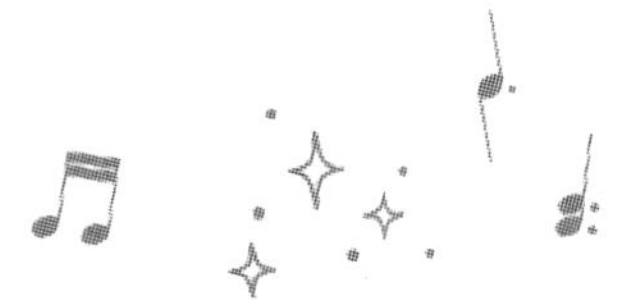

DECEMBER 24:

"We Shall See Him"

Not in that poor lowly stable,
With the oxen standing by,
We shall see Him: but in heaven,
Set at God's right hand on high,
Where like stars His children crowned,
All in white shall wait around.

–"Once in Royal David's City, "
Cecil Frances Alexander

Cecil Frances Alexander wanted to help young people learn the theology of the Apostle's Creed, and so she wrote a hymn for each phrase. "Once in Royal David's City" is based on the creed's statement that Jesus Christ was "born of the virgin Mary." Mrs. Alexander wonderfully orients our hopes properly at Christmastime, in that she doesn't leave the focus on the incarnation but moves in the conclusion of her hymn to that Great Day when Christ will come again. It is then that "we shall see him … in heaven, set at God's right hand."

This sight has been the great hope of the believer down through the ages—"in my flesh I shall see God," Job declared (Job 19:26). Paul explains the difference between life here and that life to come when he writes, "Now we see in a mirror dimly, but then face to face" (1 Cor. 13:12). The sin and selfishness, and yes, even the distance, that have blurred our vision of the ascended Christ will be removed and we will behold Him with crystal clarity: "But we know that when he appears we shall be like him, because we shall see him as he is" (1 Jn. 3:2). We will be "all in white"—perfected in holiness at long last!

This moment is sometimes referred to as the "beatific vision," literally the sight that will make us happy (*beatus* in Latin means "blessed" or "happy"). Does the prospect of seeing Jesus make you happy? Do you pray with earnestness, "Come, Lord Jesus" (Rev. 22:20)? The book of Hebrews describes Christians as those who are "eagerly waiting" for the day when Christ will "appear a second time" (9:28). Is that you? Are you eager for the return of Jesus? Many children (and adults!) are eagerly awaiting Christmas morning—"Just one more sleep!"—excited about family, food, and gifts. How much more excited we should be to see Jesus! This whole lifetime is a Second Christmas Eve—we should live filled with hopeful expectation of what that Great Day will hold for us.

This year, make sure you celebrate the incarnation in the fullest sense. That means looking back on the first coming in thankfulness, and looking ahead to the second coming in eagerness.

Pray: *Dear God, I confess that I often give little thought to the second coming of Christ. I become focused on this world and the things here that I forget my greatest hope is when I will be with my Savior and be made like Him. Help me to look forward to and live for that Day. In Jesus's name I pray. Amen.*

Reflect:

Read 1 John 3:1–3.

- What will happen when Christ comes again and we see Him face to face? How does this make you feel?
- On Christmas Eve we prepare for the big day that awaits us. What are you doing to prepare for the Great Day that awaits us at Christ's return?

DECEMBER 25:

"Joy to the World!"

Joy to the world, the Lord is come!
Let earth receive her King;
Let ev'ry heart prepare Him room
And heav'n and nature sing.

–"Joy to the World!" Isaac Watts

To have the Son of God is to have fullness of joy (Jn. 15:11)—*and we have Him*! He is here (or, in the words of Isaac Watts, He "is come"). In the incarnation, Jesus came to us. Though He is now ascended in glory, He has sent His Spirit into our hearts so that we are never apart. Moreover, even in heaven He reigns as a fully-human man. This means, in the words of an old catechism, that "we have our own flesh in heaven as a sure pledge that Christ our head will also take us, his members, up to himself."[1] Now that Christ is come, we can never be separated from Him.

This reality brings joy. And we are not talking about mere happiness here, or even extreme happiness. We are talking about the deepest, most

1 The Heidelberg Catechism, Question and Answer 49.

abiding sense of perfection and bliss and blessedness. Real joy, capital JOY, is ours forevermore. This joy is so full it cannot be contained. Psalm 98, which Mr. Watts used as the inspiration for this carol, describes the swelling joyful song sung in response to the coming King in three stanzas. In stanza one, Israel is called to sing a joyful song (based on Ps. 98:1–3); in stanza two the whole earth, even the Gentiles, are invited to join the song (vv. 4–6); in stanza three, most surprisingly, we discover that even nature can sing (vv. 7–9): "Let the rivers clap their hands; let the hills sing for joy together before the LORD, for he comes to judge the earth"!

That's peculiar, isn't it? What interest does nature have in the salvation that Christ brings to humanity? Why should "fields and floods, rocks, hills, and plains repeat the sounding joy"? Because God dwelling with mankind was always what the world was meant for. Creation was purposed to house this blessed communion between the divine and human. Ever since the Fall, the curse has made that an impossibility. But at Christmas we celebrate—and soon all nature will join us—that God has found out a way in Jesus Christ, and that indeed "the dwelling place of God is with man" (Rev. 21:3). This is joy, not just for you and me, but for the whole world.

Pray: *O great God, fill me with this joy! You have made a way for me to live with You forever, by sending Your Son and sealing me by Your Spirit. Nothing in all of creation can keep me from dwelling with You in the new heavens and new earth, when the world finally works as it was always meant to. In Jesus's name I pray. Amen.*

Reflect:

Read Psalm 98.

- Do you have a complete joy in Jesus? What does the Bible say about joy and the Christian?
- The created order will sing for joy at the return of Christ. How should this inform our praise of God?

Appendix: A New Carol, "In the Manger"

Words: Jonathan Landry Cruse, 2022
Music: IN THE MANGER | Josh Bauder, 2022